About Skill Builders
French I
Grades K–5

Welcome to Skill Builders *French I* for grades K–5. This book is designed to help children master essential French vocabulary through focused practice. This full-color workbook contains grade-level-appropriate activities based on national standards to help ensure that children master basic vocabulary before progressing.

More than 70 pages of activities cover essential vocabulary topics, such as colors and numbers, the weather, family members, and parts of the body. The book's colorful, inviting format and easy-to-follow directions help build children's confidence and make learning French more accessible and enjoyable.

The Skill Builders series offers workbooks that are perfect for keeping children current during the school year or preparing them for the next grade.

www.carsondellosa.com
Carson-Dellosa Publishing LLC
Greensboro, North Carolina

Printed in the USA • All rights reserved.

ISBN 978-1-936023-18-9
13-196191151

La table des matières (Table of Contents)

Le français dans le monde
(French Throughout the World)

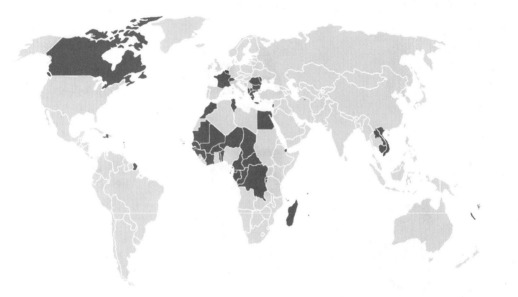

Did you know that people throughout the world speak French and have for centuries? Explorers from France have travelled the globe throughout the last 500 years, bringing with them the French language and culture.

Today, French is an official language in 29 countries. Most native French speakers live in France and other parts of Europe, including Belgium, Switzerland, and Luxembourg. You'll also find native French speakers in parts of Africa, Southeast Asia, Indonesia, and the Caribbean. The remaining French speakers live in Canada and parts of the United States, including Maine, Vermont, and Louisiana.

L'alphabet (Alphabet)

(l'alphabet)

Écrivez les lettres. (Write the letters.)

Aa
(ah)

l'ananas
(lah-nah-NAH)

Bb
(bay)

le bébé
(leh bay-BAY)

Cc
(say)

la caisse
(lah kehss)

Dd
(day)

la dent
(lah dahn)

Ee
(eh)

l'éléphant
(lay-lay-FAHN)

Ff
(ehf)

la fenêtre
(lah feh-NETR)

Gg
(zhay)

la guitare
(lah gee-TAR)

Hh
(ahsh)

la hache
(lah ahsh)

Ii
(ee)

l'insecte
(lehn-SEKT)

Jj
(zhee)

le journal
(leh zhoor-NAHL)

Kk
(kah)

le kangourou
(leh kahn-goo-ROO)

Ll
(ehl)

la lampe
(lah lahmp)

Mm
(ehm)

la maison
(lah may-ZOHN)

Écrivez les lettres. (Write the letters.)

Nn
(ehn)

la neige
(lah nehzh)

Oo
(oh)

l'océan
(loh-say-AHN)

Pp
(pay)

le pain
(leh pehn)

Qq
(qūy)

quatre
(kaht-r)

Rr
(air)

la règle
(lah REG-leh)

Ss
(ehs)

la scie
(lah see)

Tt
(tay)

la table
(lah tah-bl)

Uu
(ū)

un
uhn

Vv
(vay)

la voiture
(lah vwah-TUR)

Ww
(dūbluh vay)

le wagon
(leh wah-GOHN)

Xx
(icks)

le xylophone
(leh zee-lo-FOHN)

Yy
(eegrek)

les yeux
(lays yoo)

Zz
(zed)

le zèbre
(leh zaibr)

Les nombres (Numbers)

(lay nohm-br)

Écrivez les nombres en français. (Write the numbers in French.)

1
un
(uhn)   un

2
deux
(doo)   deux

3
trois
(twah)   trois

4
quatre
(kahtr)   quatre

5
cinq
(sank)   cinq

6
six
(seece)

six

7
sept
(set)

Sept

8
huit
(weet)

huit

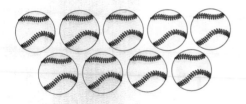

9
neuf
(noof)

neuf

10
dix
(deece)

dix

Les nombres (Numbers)

(lay nohm-br)

Écrivez les nombres en français. (Write the numbers in French.)

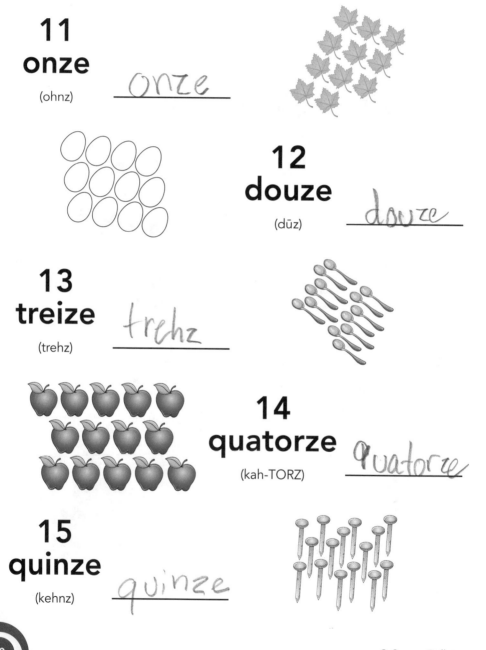

11
onze
(ohnz) _onze_

12
douze
(dūz) _douze_

13
treize
(trehz) _trehz_

14
quatorze
(kah-TORZ) _quatorze_

15
quinze
(kehnz) _quinze_

16
seize
(sehz)

seize

17
dix-sept
(deece-set)

dix-sept

18
dix-huit
(deez-weet)

dixhuit

19
dix-neuf
(deez-nŏof)

dix neœf

20
vingt
(van)

Vingt

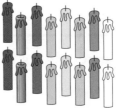

Les couleurs (Colors)
(lay ku-LUR)

Écrivez les couleurs en français. (Write the colors in French.)

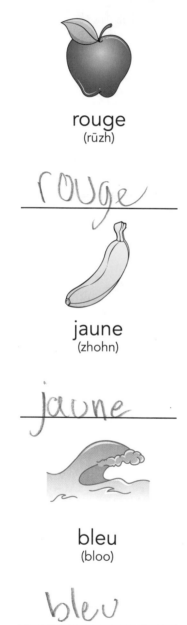

rouge
(rūzh)

rouge

orange
(o-RAHNJ)

orange

jaune
(zhohn)

jaune

vert
(vair)

vert

bleu
(bloo)

bleu

violet
(vee-oh-LAY)

violet

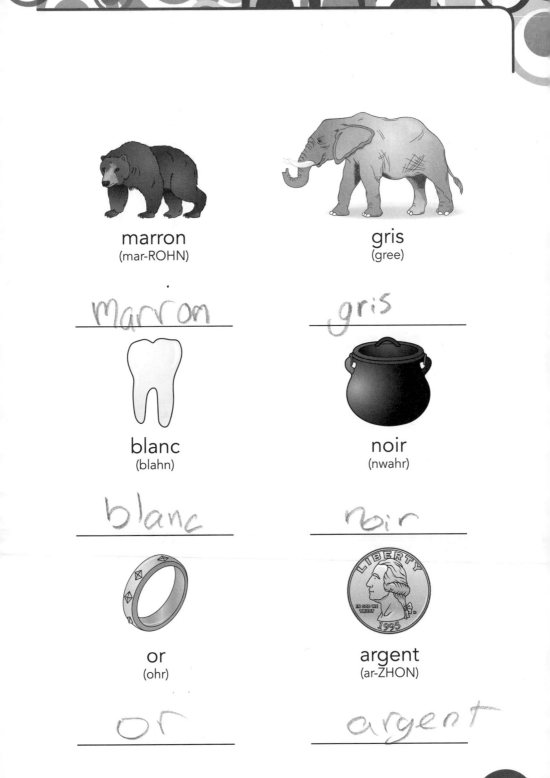

marron
(mar-ROHN)

marron

gris
(gree)

gris

blanc
(blahn)

blanc

noir
(nwahr)

noir

or
(ohr)

or

argent
(ar-ZHON)

argent

Les jours de la semaine (Days of the Week)
(lay zhur deh lah she-MEHN)

Écrivez les jours de la semaine en français.
(Write the days of the week in French.)

dimanche
(dee-mahnsh)
Sunday

dimache

lundi
(luhn-dee)
Monday

lundi

mardi
(mar-dee)
Tuesday

mardi

mercredi
(mehr-creh-dee)
Wednesday

mercredi

jeudi
(zhoo-dee)
Thursday

jeudi

vendredi
(vahn-dreh-dee)
Friday

vendrei

samedi
(sam-dee)
Saturday

Samedi

Écrivez le jour suivant. (Write the day that comes next.)

mardi _mercredi_   mercredi _jeudi_

vendredi _Samedi_   dimanche _lundi_

lundi _Mardi_   samedi _dimanche_

jeudi _vendredi_

Écrivez les mots en français. (Write the words in French.)

la semaine
(lah seh-MAHN)
(week)

la semaine

la fin de semaine
(lah FEH de seh-MAHN)
(weekend)

la fin

le mois
(leh mwah)
(month)

l'année
(lah-NAY)
(year)

l'anniversaire
(lan-nee-vair-SAIR)
(birthday)

Les mois de l'année (The Months of the Year)
(lay mwah de lah-NAY)

Écrivez les mots en français. (Write the words in French.)

janvier
(john-vee-AY)

_____

février
(fev-ree-AY)

_____

mars
(mar)

_____

avril
(av-reel)

_____

mai
(may)

_____

juin
(zhwehn)

_____

juillet
(jwee-AY)

_____

août
(oot)

_____

septembre
(set-EM-brah)

_____

octobre
(oc-TOE-brah)

_____

novembre
(no-VAHM-brah)

_____

décembre
(day-SAHM-bre)

_____

Les saisons (Seasons)
(lay say-ZOHN)

Écrivez les mots en français. (Write the words in French.)

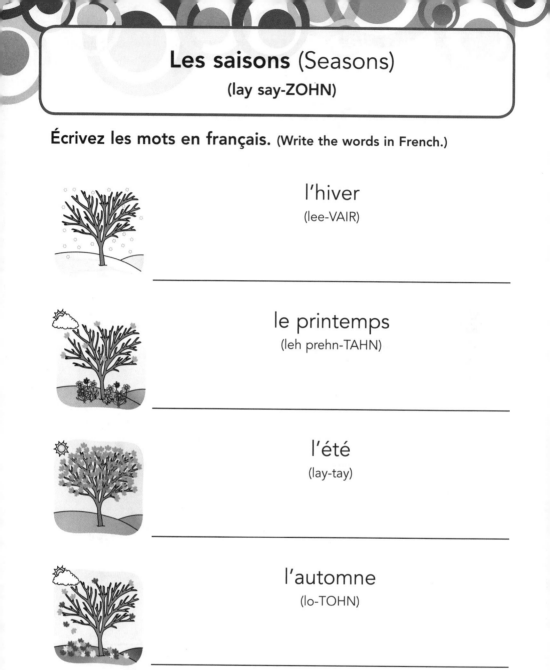

l'hiver
(lee-VAIR)

_____

le printemps
(leh prehn-TAHN)

_____

l'été
(lay-tay)

_____

l'automne
(lo-TOHN)

_____

Did you know?

France uses the euro (€), a type of currency shared by many European countries.

Le temps (Weather)
(leh tahn)

Écrivez les mots en français. (Write the words in French.)

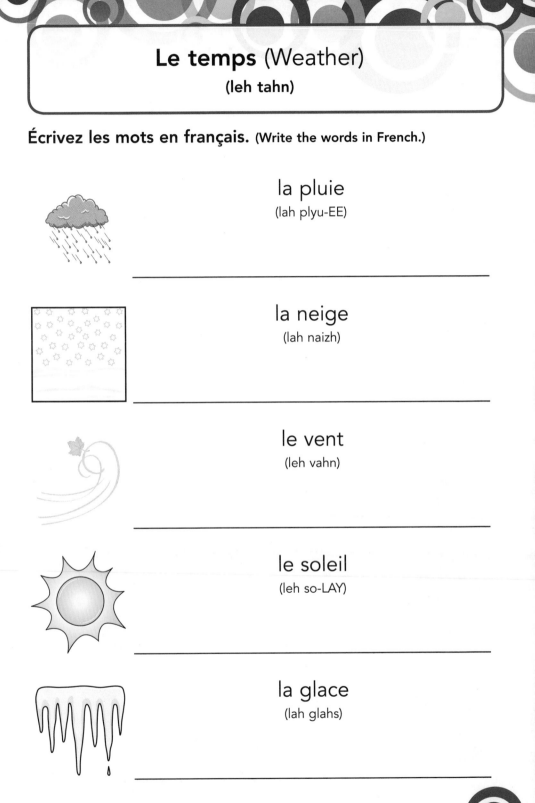

la pluie
(lah plyu-EE)

la neige
(lah naizh)

le vent
(leh vahn)

le soleil
(leh so-LAY)

la glace
(lah glahs)

Le temps (Weather)
(leh tahn)

Écrivez les mots en français. (Write the words in French.)

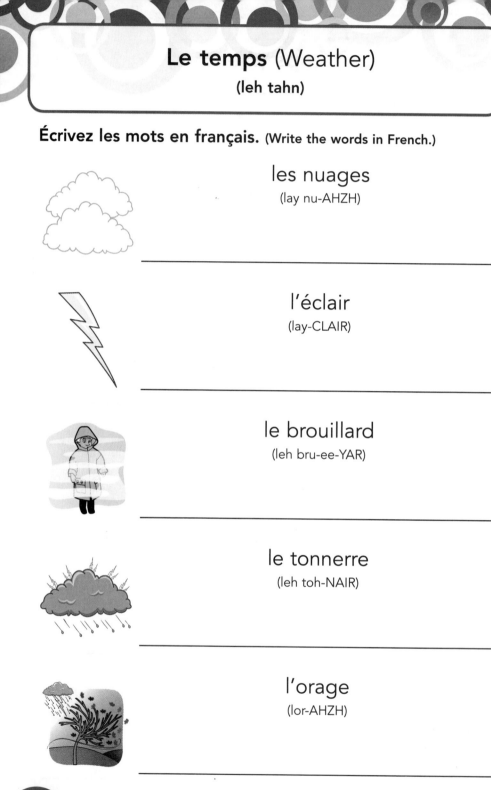

les nuages
(lay nu-AHZH)

_____

l'éclair
(lay-CLAIR)

_____

le brouillard
(leh bru-ee-YAR)

_____

le tonnerre
(leh toh-NAIR)

_____

l'orage
(lor-AHZH)

_____

Écrivez le temps et la saison en français.
(Write the weather and the season in French.)

le temps: _____   le temps: _____

la saison: _____   la saison: _____

le temps: _____   le temps: _____

la saison: _____   la saison: _____

Les animaux (Animals)
(lay-zan-ee-MO)

Écrivez les mots en français. (Write the words in French.)

le chat
(leh shah)

---

le chien
(leh she-EHN)

---

le cheval
(leh sheh-VAHL)

---

l'oiseau
(lwah-ZOH)

---

le poisson
(leh pwah-SOHN)

la vache
(lah vahsh)

la poule
(lah pool)

le canard
(leh can-ARD)

le lapin
(leh lah-PEHN)

la souris
(lah su-REE)

Did you know?

The French bulldog, the beauceron, and the basset hound all
originated in France.

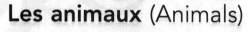

Les animaux (Animals)
(lay-zan-ee-MO)

Écrivez les mots en français. (Write the words in French.)

la chèvre
(lah shehvr)

_____

le serpent
(leh sehr-PAHN)

_____

la tortue
(lah tor-TUE)

_____

le mouton
(leh moo-TOHN)

_____

la mouche
(lah moosh)

_____

Identifiez les animaux en français. (Identify the animals in French.)

1. _____   6. _____   11. _____
2. _____   7. _____   12. _____
3. _____   8. _____   13. _____
4. _____   9. _____   14. _____
5. _____   10. _____

Les parties du corps (Parts of the Body)
(lay par-TEE du KOHR)

Écrivez les mots en français. (Write the words in French.)

la tête
(lah teht)

_____

les cheveux
(lay sheh-VOO)

_____

les yeux
(lays yoo)

_____

le nez
(leh nay)

_____

la bouche
(lah būsh)

_____

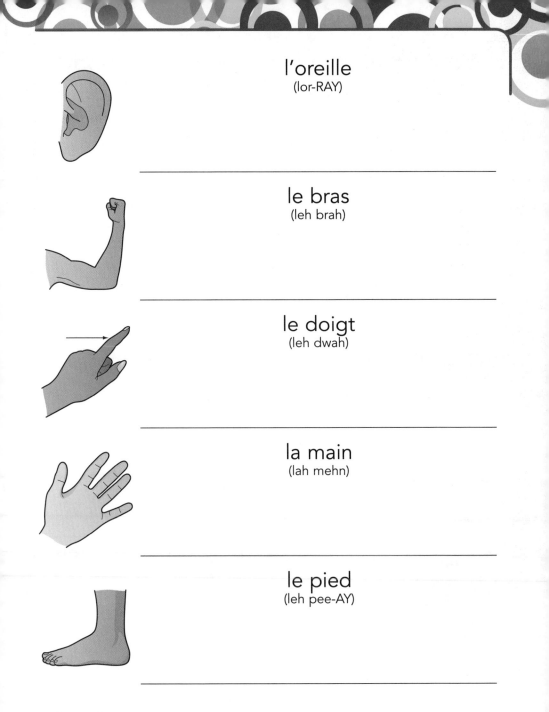

l'oreille
(lor-RAY)

le bras
(leh brah)

le doigt
(leh dwah)

la main
(lah mehn)

le pied
(leh pee-AY)

Did you know?

Bastille Day, July 14th, is France's national holiday.

Les parties du corps (Parts of the Body)
(lay par-TEE du KOHR)

Écrivez les mots en français. (Write the words in French.)

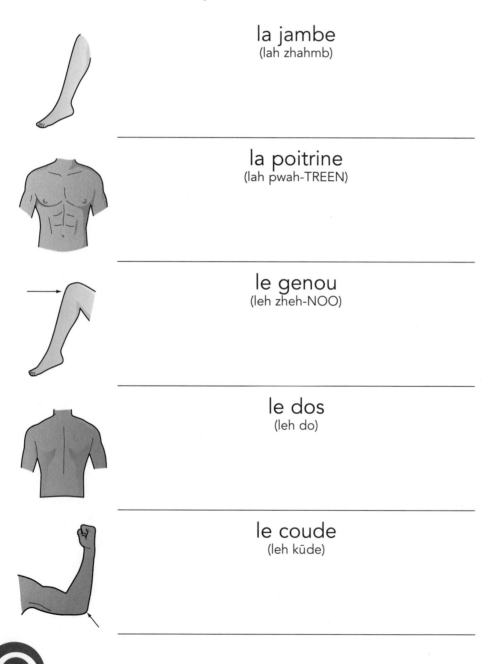

la jambe
(lah zhahmb)

_____

la poitrine
(lah pwah-TREEN)

_____

le genou
(leh zheh-NOO)

_____

le dos
(leh do)

_____

le coude
(leh kŭde)

_____

Identifiez et nommez les parties du corps en français.

(Identify and label the parts of the body in French.)

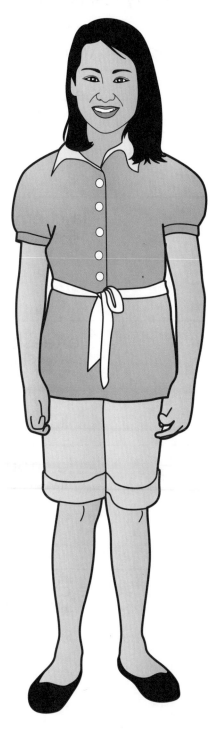

Les vêtements (Clothing)
(lay veht-MAWN)

Écrivez les mots en français. (Write the words in French.)

le pantalon
(leh pahn-tah-LOHN)

_____

la chemise
(lah shuh-MEESE)

_____

le teeshirt
(leh tee-SHIRT)

_____

le short
(leh short)

_____

le chemisier
(leh sheh-mee-ZYAY)

_____

la jupe
(lah zhyup)

les chaussures
(leh SHO-sure)

le jean
(leh jean)

les chaussettes
(lay sho-SET)

les chaussures à talon
(lay SHO-sure a ta-LOHN)

Did you know?

Paris is the capital of France... and the fashion capital of the world!

Les vêtements (Clothing)
(lay veht-MAWN)

Écrivez les mots en français. (Write the words in French.)

la veste
(lah vest)

_____

le manteau
(leh man-TOE)

_____

le pullover
(leh pool-o-VAIR)

_____

le pyjama
(leh pee-zhah-MAH)

_____

le maillot de bain
(leh my-oh duh behn)

_____

Les sports (Sports)
(lay spor)

Écrivez les mots en français. (Write the words in French.)

le base-ball
(leh bahz-BOL)

_____

le football
(leh fūt-BOL)

_____

le basket
(leh bas-KET)

_____

le hockey
(leh oh-KAY)

_____

le football américain
(le fūt-BOL ah-may-ree-KEHN)

_____

Les sports (Sports)
(lay spor)

Écrivez les mots en français. (Write the words in French.)

le tennis
(leh teh-NEES)

_____

le golf
(leh gohlf)

_____

la natation
(lah nah-tah-see-OHN)

_____

le jogging
(leh jogg-ING)

_____

le cyclisme
(leh see-kleez-MUH)

_____

le patinage
(leh pa-tee-NAHZH)

le ski
(leh skee)

le snowboard
(leh sno-BORD)

le bowling
(leh bow-LING)

l'équitation
(lay-kee-tah-see-OHN)

Did you know?

France has hosted the Olympics five times: summer 1900, winter and summer 1924, winter 1968, and winter 1992.

La famille (The Family)
(lah fah-MEEY)

Écrivez les mots en français. (Write the words in French.)

le père
(leh pair)

_____

la mère (la maman)
(lah mair) (lah mah-mahn)

_____

le fils
(leh feece)

_____

la fille
(lah feey)

_____

le frère
(leh frair)

_____

la soeur
(la ser)

le grand-père
(leh grahn-PAIR)

la grand-mère
(lah grahn-MAIR)

l'oncle
(lohn-KL)

la tante
(lah tahnt)

Did you know?

French students usually start kindergarten at age 2 or 3.

La famille (The Family)
(lah fah-MEEY)

Écrivez les mots en français. (Write the words in French.)

La maison (The House)
(lah may-ZOHN)

Écrivez les mots en français. (Write the words in French.)

la chambre
(lah shahmbr)

_____

la cuisine
(lah kwee-ZEEN)

_____

le salon
(leh sah-LOHN)

_____

la salle à manger
(lah sahl ah man-ZHAY)

_____

la salle de bains
(lah sahl de behn)

_____

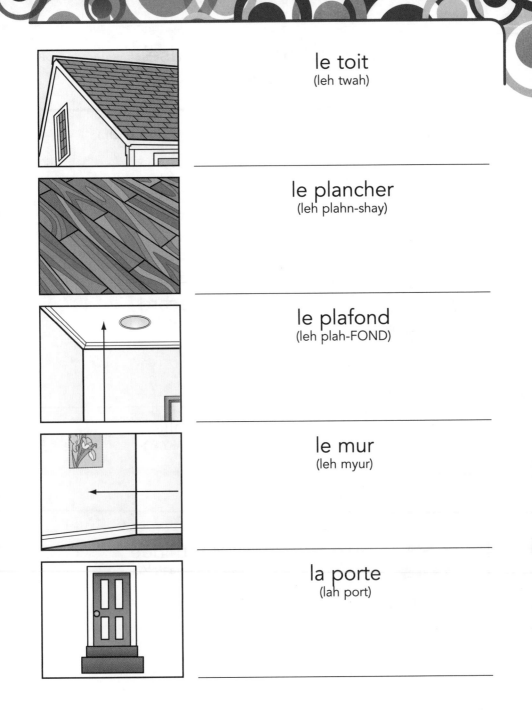

le toit
(leh twah)

le plancher
(leh plahn-shay)

le plafond
(leh plah-FOND)

le mur
(leh myur)

la porte
(lah port)

Did you know?

France is home to hundreds of historic palaces, called "châteaux."

La maison (The House)
(lah may-ZOHN)

Écrivez les mots en français. (Write the words in French.)

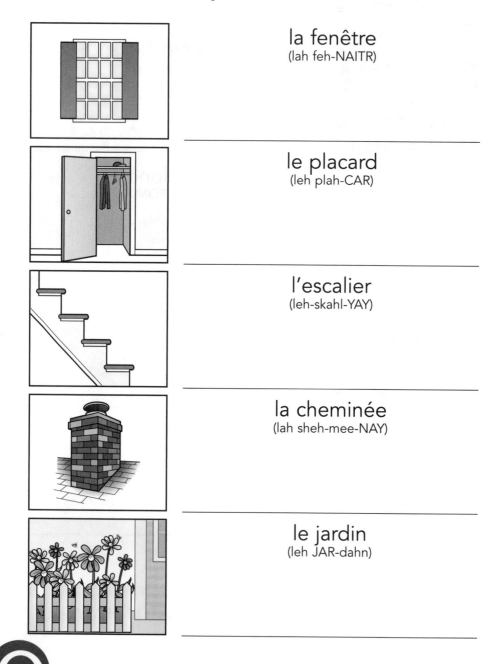

la fenêtre
(lah feh-NAITR)

le placard
(leh plah-CAR)

l'escalier
(leh-skahl-YAY)

la cheminée
(lah sheh-mee-NAY)

le jardin
(leh JAR-dahn)

Écrivez les mots en français. (Write the words in French.)

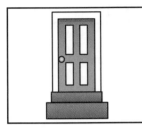  

_____ _____ _____

_____ _____ _____

_____ _____ _____

Les objets de la maison
(Objects in the House)
(lay zohb-zhay deh lah may-ZOHN)

Écrivez les mots en français. (Write the words in French.)

le canapé
(leh can-ah-PAY)

_____

la chaise
(lah shehz)

_____

la lampe
(lah lahmp)

_____

la table
(lah tahbl)

_____

le lit
(leh lee)

_____

la télévision
(lah tay-lay-vee-zee-YOHN)

le réfrigérateur
(leh reh-FRIG-er-ah-tour)

le four
(leh fūr)

l'évier
(lay-vee-ay)

la cuisinière
(lah kwee-zee-NYAIR)

Did you know?

Some French restaurants allow customers to bring their dogs inside while they dine.

Les objets de la maison
(Objects in the House)
(lay zohb-zhay deh lah may-ZOHN)

Écrivez les mots en français. (Write the words in French.)

le tapis
(leh tah-PEE)

_____

le téléphone
(leh tay-lay-FOHN)

_____

la commode
(lah koh-MOHD)

_____

l'ordinateur
(lor-DIN-ah-ter)

_____

la cheminée
(lah sheh-mee-NAY)

_____

Dessinez les objets dans la maison.
(Draw the objects in the house.)

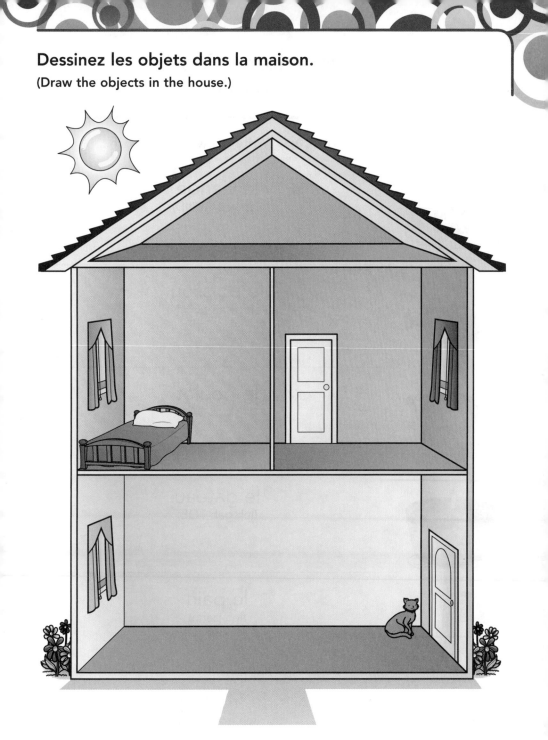

la lampe   le téléphone   la télévision   la table
l'ordinateur   la cheminée   le canapé   la chaise

La nourriture (Food)

(lah neur-i-TYUR)

Écrivez les mots en français. (Write the words in French.)

la viande
(lah vee-AHND)

_____

le poisson
(leh pwah-SOHN)

_____

le poulet
(leh poo-LAY)

_____

le gâteau
(leh gah-TOE)

_____

le pain
(leh pehn)

_____

le fromage
(leh fro-MAZH)

_____

le café
(leh ka-FAY)

_____

le thé
(leh tay)

_____

le lait
(leh lay)

_____

le jus de fruits
(leh JOO deh fru-ee)

_____

les fruits
(lay fru-ee)

_____

les légumes
(lay GOOM)

_____

La nourriture (Food)
(lah neur-i-TYUR)

Écrivez les mots en français. (Write the words in French.)

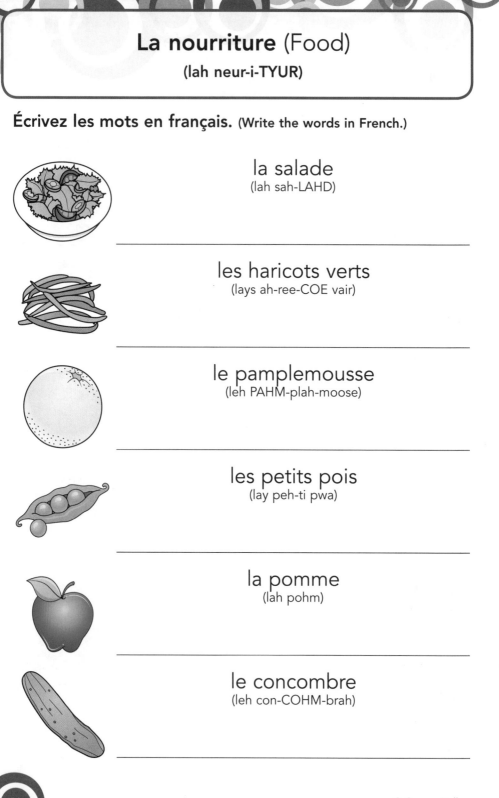

la salade
(lah sah-LAHD)

_____

les haricots verts
(lays ah-ree-COE vair)

_____

le pamplemousse
(leh PAHM-plah-moose)

_____

les petits pois
(lay peh-ti pwa)

_____

la pomme
(lah pohm)

_____

le concombre
(leh con-COHM-brah)

_____

le petit déjeuner
(leh peh-TEE day-zhun-AY)

_____

le déjeuner
(leh day-zhun-AY)

_____

le dîner
(leh dee-NAY)

_____

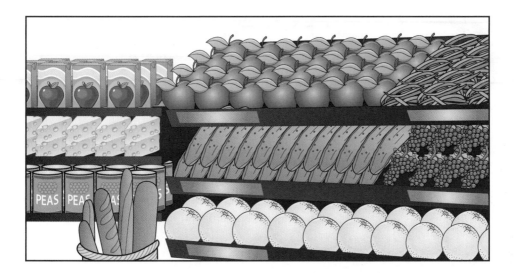

À table (At the Table)
(ah tahbl)

Écrivez les mots en français. (Write the words in French.)

le couteau
(leh ku-TOE)

_____

la fourchette
(lah fūr-SHEHT)

_____

la cuillère
(lah kyu-YAIR)

_____

l'assiette
(lass-ee-EHT)

_____

le verre
(leh vair)

_____

le bol
(leh bohl)

la tasse
(lah tahss)

la soucoupe
(lah sū-KUP)

la serviette
(lah sehr-vee-YEHT)

la nappe
(lah nahp)

Did you know?

Many people in France shop at specialty stores for everyday food items—including meat, bread, and pastries—rather than shopping at large supermarkets.

À table (At the Table)

(ah tahbl)

Écrivez ce dont on a besoin. (Write the names of the items you need to use with the following.)

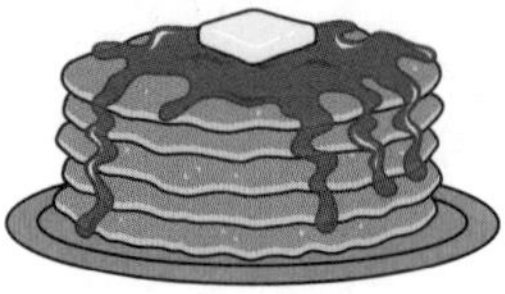

Écrivez les mots en français qui correspondent aux nombres.

(Write the words in French which correspond to the numbers.)

1. _____

2. _____

3. _____

4. _____

5. _____

6. _____

7. _____

8. _____

9. _____

10. _____

À l'école (At School)

(ah lay-KOHL)

Écrivez les mots en français. (Write the words in French.)

l'école
(lay-KOHL)

la maîtresse
(lah may-TRESS)

l'élève
(lay-LEHV)

le livre
(leh leevr)

le pupitre
(leh pyu-PEETR)

le stylo
(leh stee-loh)

la règle
(lah REG-leh)

la colle
(lah kohl)

les ciseaux
(lays SEE-soh)

le crayon
(leh kray-OHN)

le papier
(leh pah-pee-YAY)

la salle de classe
(lah sahl deh klahss)

À l'école (At School)

(ah lay-KOHL)

Écrivez les mots en français. (Write the words in French.)

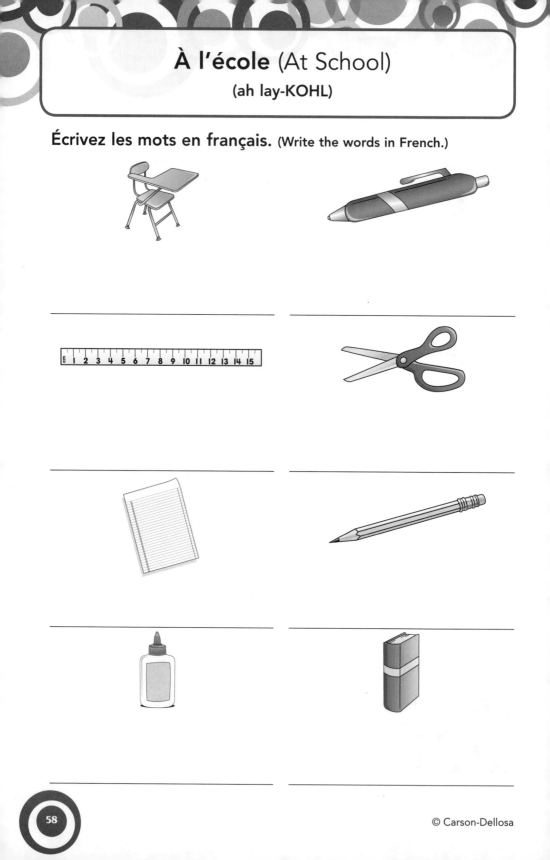

La salle de classe (The Classroom)

Écrivez les mots en français qui correspondent aux nombres.
(Write the words in French which correspond to the numbers.)

1. _____

2. _____

3. _____

4. _____

5. _____

6. _____

7. _____

8. _____

9. _____

Écrivez les mots en français. (Write the words in French.)

le policier
(leh poh-lee-see-YAY)

_____

le pompier
(leh pohn-PYAY)

_____

le plombier
(leh plohn-BYAY)

_____

le médecin
(leh mayd-SEHN)

_____

l'infirmière
(lehn-fir-mee-AIR)

_____

la dentiste
(lah dahn-TEEST)

_____

l'électricien
(lay-lehk-tree-see-EHN)

_____

le pilote
(leh pee-LOHT)

_____

la bibliothécaire
(lah BIB-lee-oh-tehk-air)

_____

le facteur
(leh fahk-TER)

_____

Did you know?

French is the national language of 29 countries, including Haiti, Switzerland, Canada, and Madagascar, and is widely spoken in more than 50 other countries.

Les professions
(People in Our Community)
(les pro-feh-see-OHN)

Écrivez les mots en français. (Write the words in French.)

le charpentier
(leh shar-pahn-tee-YAY)

_____

le camionneur
(leh ca-mee-oh-NER)

_____

le mécanicien
(leh may-cah-nee-see-EHN)

_____

la secrétaire
(lah seh-kray-TAIR)

_____

l'artiste
(lar-TEEST)

_____

Écrivez les mots en français qui correspondent aux nombres.

(Write the words in French which correspond to the numbers.)

1. _____   5. _____   9. _____

2. _____   6. _____   10. _____

3. _____   7. _____   11. _____

4. _____   8. _____   12. _____

Dans notre quartier
(Places in Our Community)
(dahn nohtr car-tee-YAY)

Écrivez les mots en français. (Write the words in French.)

l'école
(lay-KOHL)

la bibliothèque
(lah BIB-lee-oh-tehk)

le cinéma
(leh sin-EH-ma)

le parc
(leh pahrhk)

l'hôpital
(loh-pee-TAHL)

la banque
(lah bahnk)

la piscine
(lah pee-seen)

le supermarché
(leh su-per-mar-SHAY)

l'aéroport
(lair-oh-POR)

la plage
(lah plahj)

Did you know?

France has seven mountain ranges, five major river systems, and nearly 3,000 miles of seashore.

Dans notre quartier
(Places in Our Community)
(dahn nohtr car-tee-YAY)

Écrivez les mots en français. (Write the words in French.)

le restaurant
(leh res-tour-RAHN)

_____

la gare
(lah gahr)

_____

le bureau de poste
(leh bur-oh de post)

_____

le centre commercial
(leh sahn-trah com-mer-SHAHL)

_____

la boulangerie
(lah boo-LAHN-zhair-ee)

_____

D'où viennent ces personnes? Écrivez les mots en français.
(From where are these people coming? Write the words in French.)

_____ _____ _____

_____ _____ _____

_____ _____ _____

Les moyens de transport (Transportation)

(leh MOY-ehn de trans-SPOR)

Écrivez les mots en français. (Write the words in French.)

la voiture
(lah vwah-TYUR)

_____

le camion
(leh cah-mee-OHN)

_____

l'avion
(lah-vee-OHN)

_____

le bateau
(leh bah-TOE)

_____

le train
(leh trehn)

_____

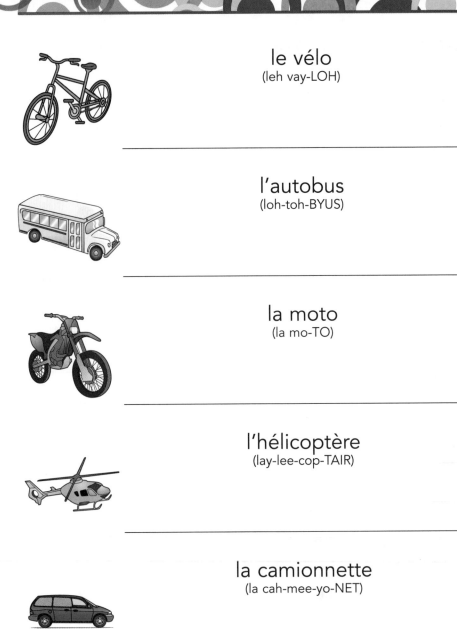

le vélo
(leh vay-LOH)

___

l'autobus
(loh-toh-BYUS)

___

la moto
(la mo-TO)

___

l'hélicoptère
(lay-lee-cop-TAIR)

___

la camionnette
(la cah-mee-yo-NET)

___

Did you know?

In France, the subway is called le métro.

Les moyens de transport (Transportation)

(leh MOY-ehn de trans-SPOR)

Dessinez le type de transport dont on a besoin dans chaque situation. Écrivez le mot en français. (Draw the type of transportation needed in each situation. Write the word in French.)

Écrivez les mots en français. (Write the words in French.)

1. Children ride on me to school.
   What am I?

2. Fishermen use me.
   What am I?

3. Time "flies" when you travel on me.
   What am I?

4. I have a caboose.
   What am I?

5. Many children learn to ride me.
   What am I?

Les paysages
(Geographical Features)
(leh PAY-yee-sahzh)

Écrivez les mots en français. (Write the words in French.)

le fleuve
(leh floov)

_____

les montagnes
(lay mohn-TAHN-yuh)

_____

l'océan
(loh-say-ahn)

_____

le lac
(leh lahk)

_____

la vallée
(lah vah-LAY)

_____

Identifez les paysages et écrivez les mots en français.

(Identify the geographical features and write the words in French.)

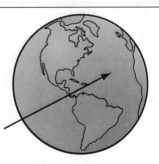

Les mots cachés (Word Search)

Trouvez les mots français cachés. (Find the hidden French words)

```
P  F  D  D  E  W  W  P  L  A  G  E  T  Q  B
B  V  G  S  P  Y  E  U  A  D  T  Q  X  G  D
F  A  V  D  U  R  R  P  L  T  Q  S  V  A  K
K  R  B  E  O  S  B  I  E  A  I  B  L  E  U
X  E  I  E  C  E  M  T  S  N  T  N  T  Y  T
E  I  R  G  U  T  A  R  S  T  M  Z  A  Q  Z
D  P  E  T  O  T  H  E  U  E  T  Y  W  G  C
K  M  N  E  S  E  C  R  O  M  R  E  N  X  E
L  O  W  H  D  S  R  H  M  M  E  A  W  G  T
C  P  K  C  H  S  W  I  E  F  I  R  V  D  I
M  C  H  N  X  U  K  Z  L  V  Z  C  H  F  W
J  P  T  A  O  A  N  Y  P  Q  E  S  T  Z  Q
O  U  S  M  T  H  V  V  M  G  N  U  G  H  D
W  V  C  I  N  C  A  N  A  R  D  T  X  L  W
P  F  F  D  G  X  J  I  P  P  G  E  B  K  Q
```

dimanche	chaussettes	chambre
canard	patinage	soucoupe
cheveux	tante	pupitre
pamplemousse	treize	plage
bleu	pompier	

Les réponses (Answer Key)

PAGE 8
1 un
2 deux
3 trois
4 quatre
5 cinq

PAGE 10
11 onze
12 douze
13 treize
14 quatorze
15 quinze

PAGE 12
rouge — (red)
orange — (orange)
jaune — (yellow)
vert — (green)
bleu — (blue)
violet — (violet)

PAGE 13
marron — (brown)
gris — (gray)
blanc — (white)
noir — (black)
or — (gold)
argent — (silver)

PAGE 14
dimanche — (Sunday)
lundi — (Monday)
mardi — (Tuesday)
mercredi — (Wednesday)
jeudi — (Thursday)
vendredi — (Friday)
samedi — (Saturday)

PAGE 15
mercredi — (Wednesday)
jeudi — (Thursday)
samedi — (Saturday)
lundi — (Monday)
mardi — (Tuesday)
dimanche — (Sunday)

PAGE 9
6 six
7 sept
8 huit
9 neuf
10 dix

PAGE 11
16 seize
17 dix-sept
18 dix-huit
19 dix-neuf
20 vingt

vendredi — (Friday)
la semaine — (week)
la fin de semaine — (weekend)
le mois — (month)
l'année — (year)
l'anniversaire — (birthday)

PAGE 16
janvier — (January)
février — (February)
mars — (March)
avril — (April)
mai — (May)
juin — (June)

PAGE 17
juillet — (July)
août — (August)
septembre — (September)
octobre — (October)
novembre — (November)
décembre — (December)

PAGE 18
l'hiver — (winter)
le printemps — (spring)
l'été — (summer)
l'automne — (fall)

PAGE 19
la pluie — (rain)
la neige — (snow)
le vent — (wind)
le soleil — (sun)
la glace — (ice)

PAGE 20
les nuages — (clouds)
l'éclair — lightning
le brouillard — (fog)
le tonnerre — (thunder)
l'orage — (storm)

Les réponses (Answer Key)

PAGE 21
Answers will vary.

le vent; la pluie;	(wind; rain;
l'orage; l'éclair	storm; lightning
(l'automne)	(fall))
le brouillard; les	(fog; clouds;
nuages; la pluie	rain (spring))
(le printemps)	
la glace; la neige	(ice; snow
(l'hiver)	(winter))
le soleil; (l'été)	(sun (summer))

PAGE 22

le chat	(cat)
le chien	(dog)
le cheval	(horse)
l'oiseau	(bird)
le poisson	(fish)

PAGE 23

la vache	(cow)
la poule	(hen)
le canard	(duck)
le lapin	(rabbit)
la souris	(mouse)

PAGE 24

la chèvre	(goat)
le serpent	(snake)
la tortue	(turtle)
le mouton	(sheep)
la mouche	(fly)

PAGE 25

1. la mouche	(fly)
2. l'oiseau	(bird)
3. le cheval	(horse)
4. la vache	(cow)
5. la poule	(hen)
6. le mouton	(sheep)
7. le chien	(dog)
8. la chèvre	(goat)
9. le lapin	(rabbit)
10. le chat	(cat)
11. le canard	(duck)
12. la tortue	(turtle)
13. le poisson	(fish)
14. le serpent	(snake)

PAGE 26

la tête	(head)
les cheveux	(hair)
les yeux	(eyes)
le nez	(nose)
la bouche	(mouth)

PAGE 27

l'oreille	(ear)
le bras	(arm)
le doigt	(finger)
la main	(hand)
le pied	(foot)

PAGE 28

la jambe	(leg)
la poitrine	(chest)
le genou	(knee)
le dos	(back)
le coude	(elbow)

PAGE 29
Order may vary, but should include:

les cheveux	(hair)
la tête	(head)
les yeux	(eyes)
l'oreille	(ear)
le nez	(nose)
la bouche	(mouth)
la poitrine	(chest)
le dos	(back)
le bras	(arm)
le coude	(elbow)
la main	(hand)
le doigt	(finger)
le genou	(knee)
la jambe	(leg)
le pied	(foot)

PAGE 30

le pantalon	(pants)
la chemise	(shirt)
le teeshirt	(t-shirt)
le short	(shorts)
le chemisier	(blouse)

Les réponses (Answer Key)

PAGE 31

la jupe	(skirt)
les chaussures	(shoes)
le jean	(jeans)
les chaussettes	(socks)
les chaussures à talon	(high heels)

PAGE 32

la veste	(jacket)
le manteau	(coat)
le pullover	(sweater)
le pyjama	(pajamas)
le maillot de bain	(swimsuit)

PAGE 33

le base-ball	(baseball)
le football	(soccer)
le basket	(basketball)
le hockey	(hockey)
le football américain	(American football)

PAGE 34

le tennis	(tennis)
le golf	(golf)
la natation	(swimming)
le jogging	(jogging)
le cyclisme	(cycling)

PAGE 35

le patinage	(ice skating)
le ski	(skiing)
le snowboard	(snowboarding)
le bowling	(bowling)
l'équitation	(horseback riding)

PAGE 36

le père	(father)
la mère/la maman	(mother)
le fils	(son)
la fille	(daughter)
le frère	(brother)

PAGE 37

la soeur	(sister)
le grand-père	(grandfather)
la grand-mère	(grandmother)
l'oncle	(uncle)
la tante	(aunt)

PAGE 38

la grand-mère	(grandmother)
la mère	(mother)
la tante	(aunt)
l'oncle	(uncle)

PAGE 39

le grand-père	(grandfather)
le père	(father)
la fille	(daughter)
le fils	(son)

PAGE 40

la chambre	(bedroom)
la cuisine	(kitchen)
le salon	(living room)
la salle à manger	(dining room)
la salle de bains	(bathroom)

PAGE 41

le toit	(roof)
le plancher	(wood floor)
le plafond	(ceiling)
le mur	(wall)
la porte	(door)

PAGE 42

la fenêtre	(window)
le placard	(closet)
l'escalier	(stairs)
la cheminée	(chimney)
le jardin	(garden)

PAGE 43

la porte	(door)
la chambre	(bedroom)
la cuisine	(kitchen)
le toit	(roof)
la cheminée	(chimney)
la salle de bains	(bathroom)
le plancher	(wood floor)
la salle à manger	(dining room)
le placard	(closet)

Les réponses (Answer Key)

PAGE 44

le canapé	(couch)
la chaise	(chair)
la lampe	(lamp)
la table	(table)
le lit	(bed)

PAGE 45

la télévision	(television)
le réfrigérateur	(refrigerator)
le four	(oven)
l'évier	(sink)
la cuisinière	(stovetop)

PAGE 46

le tapis	(rug)
le téléphone	(telephone)
la commode	(dresser)
l'ordinateur	(computer)
la cheminée	(fireplace)

PAGE 47

Students should draw the following items:

la lampe	(lamp)
le téléphone	(telephone)
la télévision	(television)
la table	(table)
l'ordinateur	(computer)
la cheminée	(fireplace)
le canapé	(couch)
la chaise	(chair)

PAGE 48

la viande	(steak)
le poisson	(fish)
le poulet	(chicken)
le gâteau	(cake)
le pain	(bread)
le fromage	(cheese)

PAGE 49

le café	(coffee)
le thé	(tea)
le lait	(milk)
le jus de fruits	(juice)

les fruits	(fruits)
les légumes	(vegetables)

PAGE 50

la salade	(salad)
les haricots verts	(green beans)
le pamplemousse	(grapefruit)
les petits pois	(peas)
la pomme	(apple)
le concombre	(cucumber)

PAGE 51

le petit déjeuner	(breakfast)
le déjeuner	(lunch)
le dîner	(dinner)

PAGE 52

le couteau	(knife)
la fourchette	(fork)
la cuillère	(spoon)
l'assiette	(plate)
le verre	(glass)

PAGE 53

le bol	(bowl)
la tasse	(cup)
la soucoupe	(saucer)
la serviette	(napkin)
la nappe	(tablecloth)

PAGE 54

Answers will vary.
la fourchette; le couteau; l'assiette (fork; knife, plate)
la cuillère; le bol (spoon; bowl)
la tasse; la soucoupe; la cuillère (cup; saucer; spoon)
le verre (glass)
la nappe; la serviette (tablecloth; napkin)

PAGE 55

1. le verre	(glass)
2. l'assiette	(plate)
3. la tasse	(cup)
4. la soucoupe	(saucer)
5. le bol	(bowl)

Les réponses (Answer Key)

6. la serviette   (napkin)
7. la nappe   (tablecloth)
8. la fourchette   (fork)
9. le couteau   (knife)
10. la cuillère   (spoon)

PAGE 56
l'école   (school)
la maîtresse   (teacher)
l'élève   (pupil)
le livre   (book)
le pupitre   (desk)
le stylo   (pen)

PAGE 57
la règle   (ruler)
la colle   (glue)
les ciseaux   (scissors)
le crayon   (pencil)
le papier   (paper)
la salle de classe   (classroom)

PAGE 58
le pupitre   (desk)
le stylo   (pen)
la règle   (ruler)
les ciseaux   (scissors)
le papier   (paper)
le crayon   (pencil)
la colle   (glue)
le livre   (textbook)

PAGE 59
1. l'élève   (pupil)
2. la maîtresse   (teacher)
3. le livre   (book)
4. la colle   (glue)
5. les ciseaux   (scissors)
6. le papier   (paper)
7. le crayon   (pencil)
8. la règle   (ruler)
9. le pupitre   (desk)

PAGE 60
le policier   (police officer)
le pompier   (firefighter)
le plombier   (plumber)

le médecin   (doctor)
l'infirmière   (nurse)

PAGE 61
la dentiste   (dentist)
l'électricien   (electrician)
le pilote   (pilot)
la bibliothécaire   (librarian)
le facteur   (mail carrier)

PAGE 62
le charpentier   (carpenter)
le camionneur   (truck driver)
le mécanicien   (mechanic)
la secrétaire   (secretary)
l'artiste   (artist)

PAGE 63
1. le pilote   (pilot)
2. l'artiste   (artist)
3. la dentiste   (dentist)
4. le médecin   (doctor)
5. l'infirmière   (nurse)
6. la secrétaire   (secretary)
7. la bibliothécaire   (librarian)
8. le charpentier   (carpenter)
9. le facteur   (mail carrier)
10. le mécanicien   (mechanic)
11. le policier   (police officer)
12. le camionneur   (truck driver)

PAGE 64
l'école   (school)
la bibliothèque   (library)
le cinéma   (movie theatre)
le parc   (park)
l'hôpital   (hospital)

PAGE 65
la banque   (bank)
la piscine   (pool)
le supermarché   (supermarket)
l'aéroport   (airport)
la plage   (beach)

Les réponses (Answer Key)

PAGE 66
le restaurant	(restaurant)
la gare	(train station)
le bureau de poste	(post office)
le centre commercial	(shopping mall)
la boulangerie	(bakery)

PAGE 67
la bibliothèque	(library)
la plage	(beach)
le centre commercial	(shopping mall)
le bureau de poste	(post office)
la boulangerie	(bakery)
l'école	(school)
la piscine	(pool)
le cinéma	(movie theatre)
l'hôpital	(hospital)

PAGE 68
la voiture	(car)
le camion	(truck)
l'avion	(plane)
le bateau	(boat)
le train	(train)

PAGE 69
le vélo	(bicycle)
l'autobus	(bus)
la moto	(motorcycle)
l'hélicoptère	(helicopter)
la camionnette	(van)

PAGE 70
l'autobus	(bus)
le camion	(truck)
l'avion	(plane)
le bateau	(boat)
le vélo	(bicycle)
le train	(train)

PAGE 71
1. l'autobus	(bus)
2. le bateau	(boat)
3. l'avion	(airplane)
4. le train	(train)
5. le vélo	(bicycle)

PAGE 72
le fleuve	(river)
les montagnes	(mountains)
l'océan	(ocean)
le lac	(lake)
la vallée	(valley)

PAGE 73
les montagnes	(mountains)
l'océan	(ocean)
le lac	(lake)
le fleuve	(river)
les montagnes	(mountains)
le fleuve	(river)
le lac	(lake)
l'océan	(ocean)

PAGE 74
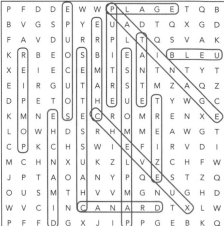